Draw a SQUARE Draw ANYTHING!

Chris Hart

Draw a SQUARE Draw ANYTHING!

LEARN TO DRAW STARTING WITH SIMPLE SHAPES

Chris Hart Books

An imprint of
Sixth & Spring Books
233 Spring St.
New York, NY 10013

Editorial Director
ELAINE SILVERSTEIN

Book Division Manager
WENDY WILLIAMS

Senior Editor
MICHELLE BREDESON

Copy Editor
KRISTINA SIGLER

Art Director
DIANE LAMPHRON

Associate Art Director
SHEENA T. PAUL

Book Design
NANCY SABATO

Vice President, Publisher
TRISHA MALCOLM

Production Manager
DAVID JOINNIDES

Creative Director
JOE VIOR

President
ART JOINNIDES

Library of Congress Control Number:
2 0 0 8 9 2 5 0 3 5
I S B N - 1 3 : 9 7 8 - 1 - 9 3 3 0 2 7 - 7 0 - 8
I S B N - 1 0 : 1 - 9 3 3 0 2 7 - 7 0 - 3
MANUFACTURED IN CHINA

1   3   5   7   9   10   8   6   4   2

First Edition

 **chrishartbooks.com**

Learning to draw has never been so EASY, or so much FUN!

Can you draw a [ ] ? Then you can draw anything!

Would you like to draw a cuddly ?

How about a blasting into space?

Or a fire-breathing ?

You'll learn how to draw all of them + a grumpy ,

a caped and lots more cool characters and

wacky animals. We'll start off every picture with a [ ]

and add to it, little by little, to end up with a finished drawing.

Happy Drawing!

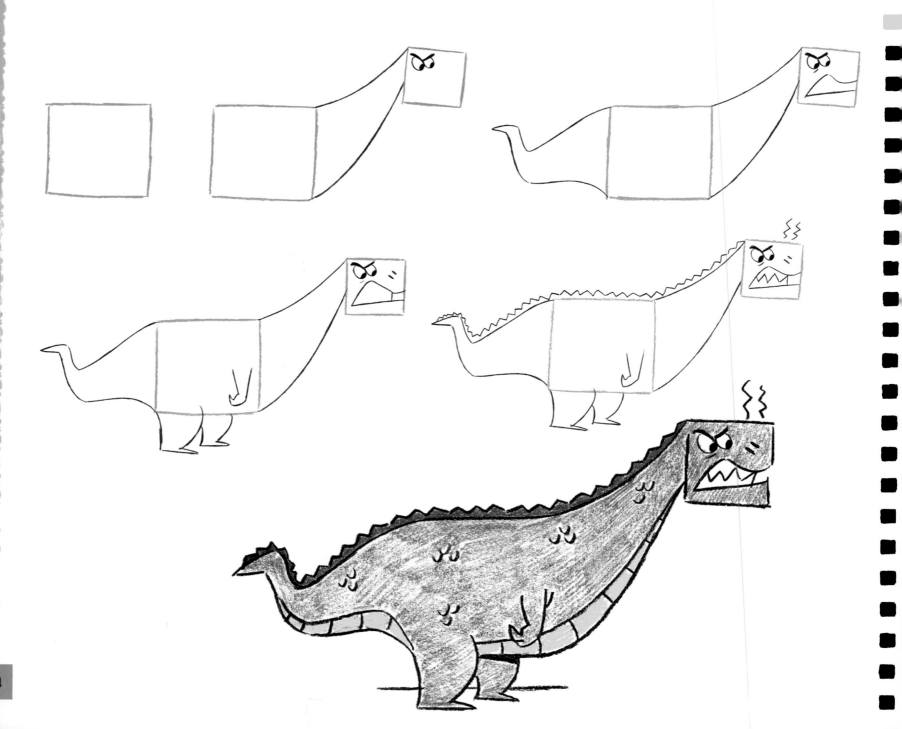

29

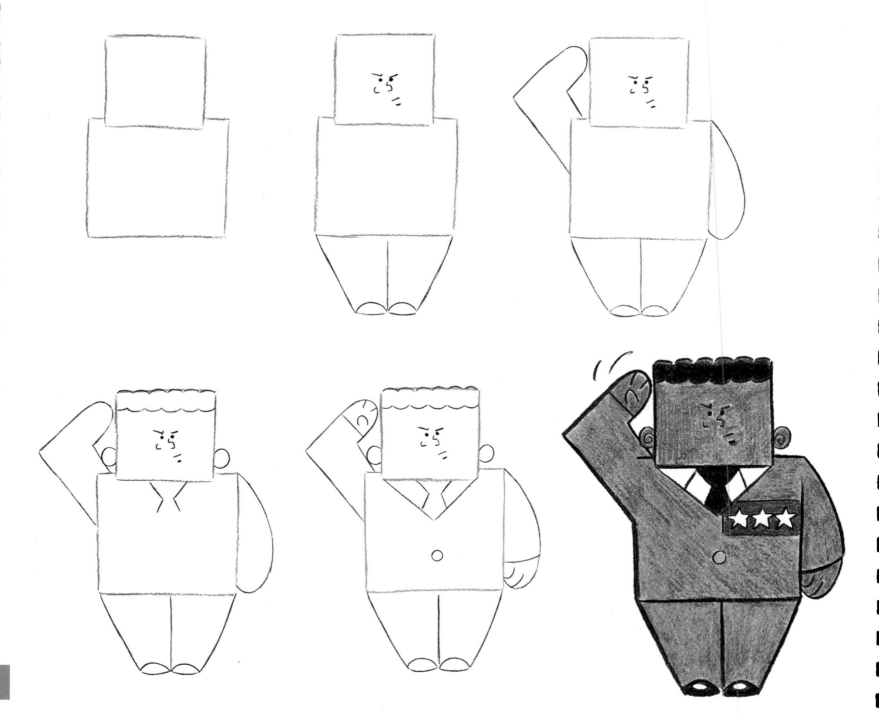

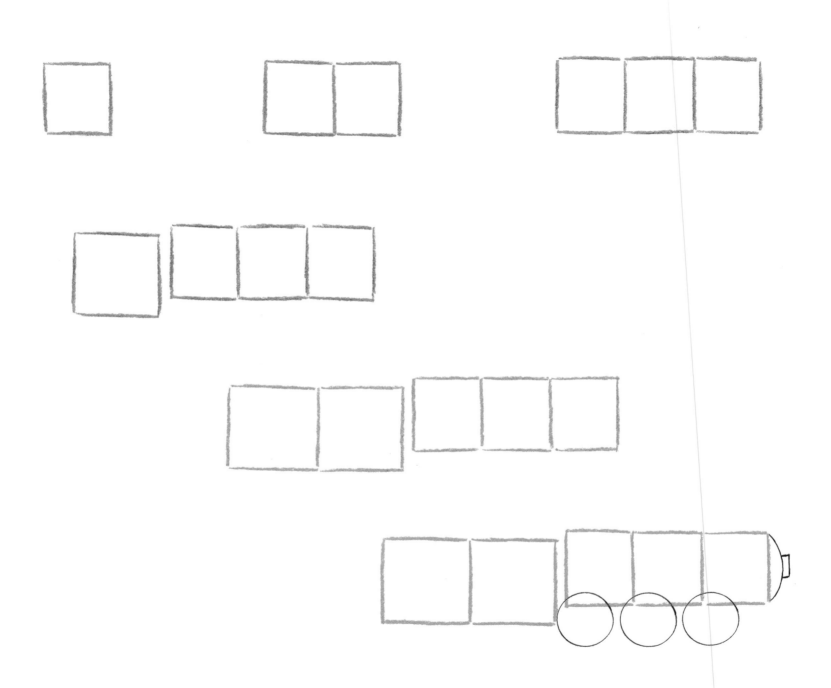

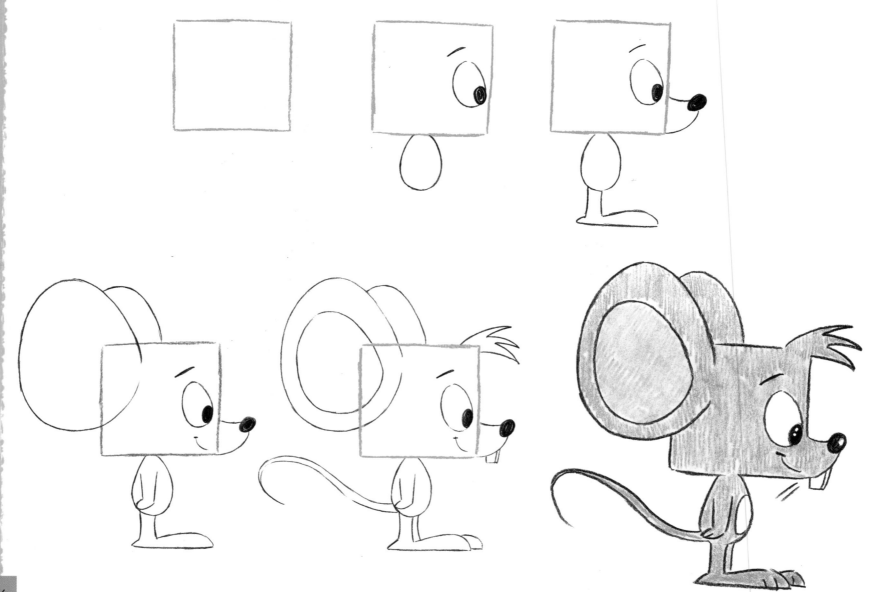

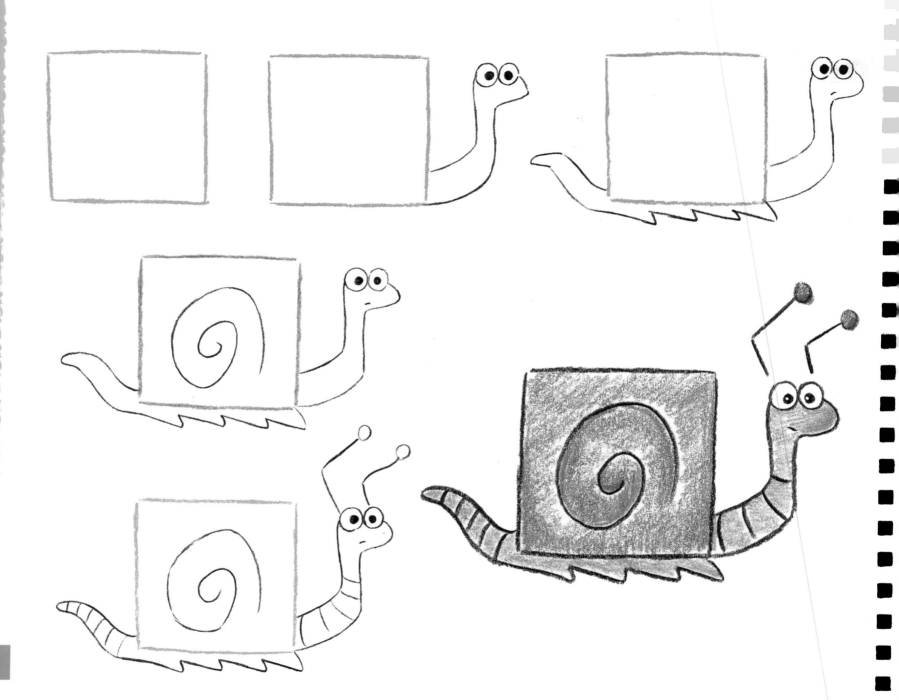

52

53

Chris Hart Books
FOR KIDS

Draw a TRIANGLE
Draw ANYTHING!

Learn to Draw starting with Simple Shapes

Chris Hart Books
FOR KIDS

Draw a CIRCLE
Draw ANYTHING!

Learn to Draw starting with Simple Shapes

Available at bookstores or online at chrishartbooks.com